Bon Appetit – French Recipes with an Accent

Dishes that Celebrate the Genuine Love of France

By: Layla Tacy

D1385270

License Notes

Table of Contents

Introduction

French food is rich, creamy and delicate and has a symphony of flavors like the country, and in this recipe book, there is a fewer selection but truly unique to France. Whether you are out eating out at restaurants or sniffing in the aromas at pastry shop windows, France is home to delicious food that makes you want to be a chef.

These 30 recipes are your guide to French home cooking that will wow your family and friends.

XXXXXXXXXXXXXXXXXXXXXXXXXXXXXXXXXXXXXXXXXXXXXXXXXXXXXXXXXXXX

Pasta Recipes

XXXXXXXXXXXXXXXXXXXXXXXXXXXXXXXXXXXXXXXXXXXXXXXXXXXXXXXXXXXX

Recipe 1: Zucchini and Chicken Pasta

Duration: 20 minutes

Serve: 2

Ingredient List:

- 2 tablespoons Oil
- 2 cups Leek (sliced)
- 2 Garlic cloves (chopped)
- 1 cup Flour
- 2 tablespoons Chicken stock
- 1 lb. Chicken (shredded)
- 5 cups Pasta
- 2 Zucchini (chopped)
- 2 cups Cheese (grated)

xxxxxxxxxxxxxxxxxxxxxxxxxxxxxxxxxxxxxxxxxxxxxxxxxxxxxxxxx

How to Cook:

1. Add oil and leek into the bowl.

2. Mix garlic, flour, chicken stock, chicken, zucchini and cheese.

3. Heat the pan lightly and add the mixture to cook for 5 minutes.

4. Add pasta and cook for 15 more minutes.

5. When ready, serve and enjoy!

Recipe 2: Tomato Spaghetti

Duration: 10 minutes.

Serve: 3

Ingredient List:

- 2 tablespoons Oil
- 2 Garlic cloves (crushed)
- 1 Onion (sliced)
- 1 small pack Spaghetti
- 2 tablespoons Tomato paste
- 2 Tomatoes (crushed)
- Salt and pepper to taste
- 1 tablespoon Sugar
- 1 tablespoon Basil (chopped)
- 1 tablespoon Parsley (chopped)

xxxxxxxxxxxxxxxxxxxxxxxxxxxxxxxxxxxxxxxxxxxxxxxxxxxxxxxxxx

How to Cook:

1. Add oil into the lightly heated pan.

2. Mix garlic, onion, tomato paste, tomatoes, sugar, basil, parsley with salt and pepper.

3. Cook for 10 minutes.

4. Meanwhile, boil spaghetti.

5. When ready, mix both and serve!

Recipe 3: Spicy Mix Spaghetti

Duration: 10 minutes

Serve: 3

Ingredient List:

- 1 tablespoon Olive oil
- 1 Onion (chopped)
- 1 Garlic clove (chopped)
- ½ tablespoons Red chili powder
- 1 tablespoon Tomato paste
- 1 small pack Spaghetti
- 2 Tomatoes
- 1 tablespoon Balsamic vinegar
- 2 Baby rocket leaves

xxxxxxxxxxxxxxxxxxxxxxxxxxxxxxxxxxxxxxxxxxxxxxxxxxxxxxx

How to Cook:

1. Add oil into the pan.

2. Mix onion, garlic, red chili powder, tomato paste, tomatoes, balsamic vinegar and rocket leaves.

3. Cook for 10 minutes.

4. Meanwhile, boil spaghetti.

5. When ready, mix both and serve!

Recipe 4: Rigate with Parsley

Duration: 10 minutes

Serve: 3

Ingredient List:

- 1 small pack Penne Rigate
- 2 tablespoons Olive oil
- 2 Onions (chopped)
- 1 Long red chili
- 2 cups Mushrooms (chopped)
- 2 tablespoons Pasta sauce
- 2 tablespoons Wine vinegar
- 1 lb. Cooked tuna
- 1 cup Parsley (chopped)
- Salt and pepper to taste

xxxxxxxxxxxxxxxxxxxxxxxxxxxxxxxxxxxxxxxxxxxxxxxxxxxxxxxxxx

How to Cook:

1. Add oil into the pan.

2. Mix onion, red chili, mushrooms, pasta sauce, wine vinegar, tuna, parsley with salt and pepper.

3. Cook for 10 minutes.

4. Meanwhile, boil Rigate.

5. When ready, mix both and serve!

Recipe 5: Kale Baked Pasta

Duration: 25 minutes

Serve: 3

Ingredient List:

- 2 tablespoons Butter
- 2 Onions (chopped)
- 2 Garlic cloves (chopped)
- 2 cups Thyme (chopped)
- 2 cups Cauliflower (chopped)
- 2 cups Full cream
- 2 tablespoons Oil
- 2 cups Kale (chopped)
- 5 cups Pasta
- 2 cups Cheese (grated)

xxxxxxxxxxxxxxxxxxxxxxxxxxxxxxxxxxxxxxxxxxxxxxxxxxxxxx

How to Cook:

1. Add butter and onion into the bowl.

2. Mix garlic, thyme, cauliflower, full cream, oil, kale and cheese.

3. Heat the oven to 350 and place the pasta as a base into the baking tray,

4. Pour the mixture and cover.

5. Bake for 25 minutes.

6. When ready, serve and enjoy!

Recipe 6: Basil Pasta

Duration: 15 minutes

Serve: 2

Ingredient List:

- 2 tablespoons Oil
- 1 Onion (chopped)
- 2 Garlic cloves (minced)
- 2 Tomatoes (chopped)
- 1 small pack Pasta
- 2 tablespoons Sugar
- 1 cup Basil leaves

XXXXXXXXXXXXXXXXXXXXXXXXXXXXXXXXXXXXXXXXXXXXXXXXXXXXXXXXX

How to Cook:

1. Add oil into the lightly heated pan.

2. Mix onion, garlic, tomatoes, sugar and basil leaves.

3. Cook for 10 minutes.

4. Meanwhile, boil the pasta.

5. When ready, mix both and serve!

Recipe 7: Quick Pasta with Herbs

Duration: 20 minutes

Serve: 2

Ingredient List:

- 2 tablespoons Olive oil
- 1 Onion (chopped)
- 2 Garlic cloves (minced)
- 2 tablespoons Tomato paste
- 2 Tomatoes (crushed)
- 1 tablespoon Dried herbs mix
- 1 small pack Pasta

xxxxxxxxxxxxxxxxxxxxxxxxxxxxxxxxxxxxxxxxxxxxxxxxxxxxxxx

How to Cook:

1. Lightly heat the pan and add oil.

2. Mix onion, garlic, tomato paste, tomatoes and herbs.

3. Cook for 10 minutes

4. Meanwhile boil pasta.

5. When ready, mix both and serve.

Recipe 8: Chicken Stock Pasta

Duration: 15 minutes

Serve: 3

Ingredient List:

- 2 tablespoons Butter
- 2 tablespoons Oil
- 2 Potatoes (chopped)
- 2 cups Chicken stock
- 2 Tomatoes (diced)
- 1 small pack Pasta
- 4 cups Water
- 2 cups Basil leaves (chopped)

xxxxxxxxxxxxxxxxxxxxxxxxxxxxxxxxxxxxxxxxxxxxxxxxxxxxxxxxxxx

How to Cook:

1. Add oil into the pot.

2. Mix butter, potatoes, chicken stock, tomatoes, water and basil leaves.

3. Cook for 15 minutes.

4. Meanwhile, boil pasta.

5. When ready, add pasta into the pot and serve!

Recipe 9: Pork Sausage Pasta

Duration: 25 minutes

Serve: 2

Ingredient List:

- 2 tablespoons Olive oil
- 2 Onions (chopped)
- 2 Garlic cloves (minced)
- 1 lb. Italian pork sausages
- 2 tablespoons White wine
- 2 Tomatoes (diced)
- 1 small pack Pasta
- 2 cups Parmesan cheese (shredded)
- 2 cups Basil leaves (chopped)

xxxxxxxxxxxxxxxxxxxxxxxxxxxxxxxxxxxxxxxxxxxxxxxxxxxxxxxxx

How to Cook:

1. Add garlic and onion into the bowl.

2. Mix oil, Italian pork sausages, white wine, tomatoes, parmesan cheese and basil leaves.

3. Heat the oven to 350F and place the pasta as a base into the baking tray,

4. Pour the mixture and cover with the pasta again.

5. Bake for 25 minutes.

6. When ready, serve and enjoy!

Lasagna Recipes

xxxxxxxxxxxxxxxxxxxxxxxxxxxxxxxxxxxxxxxxxxxxxxxxxxxxxxxxxxx

Recipe 10: Pumpkin Lasagna

Duration: 25 minutes

Serve: 3

Ingredient List:

- 1 lb. Butternut pumpkin (sliced)
- 2 tablespoons Oil
- 1 Zucchini (chopped)
- 2 Garlic cloves (chopped)
- 2 tablespoons Cinnamon powder
- 2 tablespoons Allspice powder
- 2 Tomatoes (chopped)
- 2 tablespoons Oregano leaves (chopped)
- 2 cups Ricotta cheese
- 5 Lasagna sheets

xxxxxxxxxxxxxxxxxxxxxxxxxxxxxxxxxxxxxxxxxxxxxxxxxxxxxxxxxxx

How to Cook:

1. Add oil and pumpkin into the bowl.

2. Mix zucchini, garlic, cinnamon, allspice, tomatoes, oregano and cheese.

3. Heat the oven to 350F and place the lasagna sheets as a base into the baking tray,

4. Pour the mixture and cover with the sheets again.

5. Bake for 25 minutes.

6. When ready, serve and enjoy!

Recipe 11: Beef Lasagna

Duration: 25 minutes

Serve: 2

Ingredient List:

- 2 tablespoons Oil
- 1 lb. Beef (minced)
- 1 Carrot (chopped)
- 1 Zucchini (chopped)
- 2 Red capsicums (chopped)
- 1 cup Basil (chopped)
- 5 Lasagna sheets
- 1 cup Cheese (grated)
- 2 tablespoons Lasagna sauce

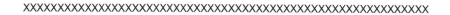

xxxxxxxxxxxxxxxxxxxxxxxxxxxxxxxxxxxxxxxxxxxxxxxxxxxxxxxxx

How to Cook:

1. Add oil and beef into the bowl.

2. Mix carrot, zucchini, red capsicums, basil and cheese with lasagna sauce.

3. Heat the oven to 350F and place the sheets as a base into the baking tray,

4. Pour the mixture and cover with the sheets again.

5. Bake for 25 minutes.

6. When ready, serve!

Recipe 12: Pork Sausage Lasagna

Duration: 25 minutes

Serve: 2

Ingredient List:

- 2 tablespoons Olive oil
- 2 Onions (chopped)
- 2 Garlic cloves (minced)
- 1 lb. Italian pork sausages
- 2 tablespoons White wine
- 2 Tomatoes (diced)
- 1 small pack Lasagna sheet
- 2 cups Parmesan cheese (shredded)
- 2 cups Basil leaves (chopped)

How to Cook:

1. Add garlic and onion into the bowl.

2. Mix oil, Italian pork sausages, white wine, tomatoes, parmesan cheese and basil leaves.

3. Heat the oven to 350F and place the lasagna sheets as a base into the baking tray,

4. Pour the mixture and cover with the sheets again.

5. Bake for 25 minutes.

6. When ready, serve and enjoy!

Recipe 13: Spinach and Ham Lasagna

Duration: 20 minutes

Serve: 3

Ingredient List:

- 2 tablespoons Oil
- 2 Onions (chopped)
- 2 Garlic cloves (chopped)
- 2 Tomatoes (chopped)
- 3 cups Spinach
- 1 lb. Ham (sliced)
- 4 Lasagna sheets
- 2 cups Cheese (grated)
- 2 cups Parsley (chopped)

xxxxxxxxxxxxxxxxxxxxxxxxxxxxxxxxxxxxxxxxxxxxxxxxxxxxxxxxxxx

How to Cook:

1. Add oil into the bowl.

2. Mix onion, garlic, tomatoes, spinach, ham and cheese.

3. Heat the oven to 350 F and put the lasagna sheets at the bottom of the baking tray.

4. Pour the mixture and cover with the sheets again.

5. Bake for 20 minutes.

6. When ready, serve!

Recipe 14: Asparagus Mix Lasagna

Duration: 25 minutes

Serve: 2

Ingredient List:

- 2 tablespoons Oil
- 2 Onions (chopped)
- 2 Garlic cloves (chopped)
- 1 lb. Chicken (minced)
- 2 tablespoons Water
- 2 tablespoons White wine
- 2 tablespoons Thyme leaves (chopped)
- 2 tablespoons Chicken stock
- 2 tablespoons Lemon rind (grated)
- 2 cups Flour
- 5 Lasagna sheets
- 4 Asparagus (chopped)
- 2 tablespoons Pine nuts (chopped)

xxxxxxxxxxxxxxxxxxxxxxxxxxxxxxxxxxxxxxxxxxxxxxxxxxxxxxxxxx

How to Cook:

1. Add onion and oil into the bowl.

2. Mix garlic, chicken, water, white wine, thyme, chicken stock, lemon rind, butter, and asparagus with pine nuts.

3. Heat the oven to 350F and place the lasagna sheets as a base into the baking tray,

4. Pour the mixture and cover with the sheets again.

5. Bake for 25 minutes.

6. When ready, serve and enjoy!

Recipe 15: Kale lasagna

Duration: 25 minutes

Serve: 3

Ingredient List:

- 2 tablespoons Butter
- 2 Onions (chopped)
- 2 Garlic cloves (chopped)
- 2 cups Thyme (chopped)
- 2 cups Cauliflower (chopped)
- 2 cups Full cream
- 2 tablespoons Oil
- 2 cups Kale (chopped)
- 5 Lasagna sheets
- 2 cups Cheese (grated)

xxxxxxxxxxxxxxxxxxxxxxxxxxxxxxxxxxxxxxxxxxxxxxxxxxxxxxxxx

How to Cook:

1. Add butter and onion into the bowl.

2. Mix garlic, thyme, cauliflower, full cream, oil, kale and cheese.

3. Heat the oven to 350F and place the lasagna sheets as a base into the baking tray,

4. Pour the mixture and cover with the sheets again.

5. Bake for 25 minutes.

6. When ready, serve and enjoy!

Recipe 16: Kidney Bean Lasagna

Duration: 30 minutes

Serve: 3

Ingredient List:

- 2 tablespoons Oil
- 2 Celery stalks (sliced)
- 1 Onion (chopped)
- 1 Carrot (chopped)
- 2 Garlic cloves (minced)
- 1 tablespoon Chili flakes
- 2 tablespoons Cumin powder
- 2 tablespoons Cinnamon powder
- 2 tablespoons Tomato paste
- 2 Tomatoes (chopped)
- 2 cups Kidney beans (cooked)
- 2 cups Sour cream
- 5 Lasagna sheets

xxxxxxxxxxxxxxxxxxxxxxxxxxxxxxxxxxxxxxxxxxxxxxxxxxxxxxxxxxx

How to Cook:

1. Add oil and celery into the bowl.

2. Mix onion, carrot, garlic, chili flakes, cumin powder, cinnamon powder, tomato paste, tomatoes, kidney beans and sour cream.

3. Heat the oven to 350F and place the lasagna sheets as a base into the baking tray,

4. Pour the mixture and cover with the sheets again.

5. Bake for 30 minutes.

6. When ready, serve and enjoy!

Recipe 17: Pork and Mushroom Lasagna

Duration: 25 minutes

Serve: 2

Ingredient List:

- 2 tablespoons Oil
- 2 Onions (chopped)
- 2 Garlic cloves (chopped)
- 1 lb. Mushrooms (sliced)
- 1 lb. Pork (minced)
- 2 tablespoons Passata sauce
- 1 cup Basil leaves (chopped)
- 4 Lasagna sheets
- 2 cups Sauce (any)
- 2 cups Cheese (grated)

xxxxxxxxxxxxxxxxxxxxxxxxxxxxxxxxxxxxxxxxxxxxxxxxxxxxxxxx

How to Cook:

1. Add onion and oil into the bowl.

2. Mix garlic, mushrooms, pork, Passata sauce, basil leaves, sauce and cheese.

3. Heat the oven to 350F and place the lasagna sheets as a base into the baking tray,

4. Pour the mixture and cover with the sheets again.

5. Bake for 25 minutes.

6. When ready, serve and enjoy!

Dessert Recipes

xxxxxxxxxxxxxxxxxxxxxxxxxxxxxxxxxxxxxxxxxxxxxxxxxxxxxxxxxx

Recipe 18: Chocolate Cream Balls

Duration: 20 minutes

Serve: 2-3

Ingredient List:

- 1 cup Heavy cream
- 2 tablespoons Corn syrup
- 2 tablespoons Unsalted butter
- 2 big bars Milk chocolate (chopped)
- 1 cup Cocoa powder
- 2 tablespoons Cardamom powder

xxxxxxxxxxxxxxxxxxxxxxxxxxxxxxxxxxxxxxxxxxxxxxxxxxxxxxxx

How to Cook:

1. Add heavy cream and corn syrup into a bowl. Mix well.

2. Now blend butter, milk chocolate and cardamom powder in the same bowl.

3. When it turns into a thick texture, make small balls and place it in the fridge for 20 minutes.

4. Sprinkle cocoa powder on the top and serve to enjoy the creamy dessert.

Recipe 19: Cocoa Powder Bites

Duration: 10 minutes

Serve: 2-3

Ingredient List:

- 2 cups Chocolate (chopped)
- 1 ½ cups Butter
- ½ teaspoons Salt
- 2 Egg yolks
- 1 cup Cocoa powder

How to Cook:

1. Add butter, salt and egg yolks into the bowl.

2. Blend well while adding chocolate and cocoa powder.

3. Heat the oven to 300 F and pour the mixture into the baking dish.

4. Let it bake for 10 minutes.

5. When done, cut it into small rectangular pieces and dress it with cocoa powder to serve!

Recipe 20: Maple Syrup Mix Dessert

Duration: 15 minutes

Serve: 2-3

Ingredient List:

- 1 cup Maple syrup
- 2 cups Flour
- 3 teaspoons Baking powder
- ½ teaspoons Salt
- 4 tablespoons Butter
- 1 cup Milk

xxxxxxxxxxxxxxxxxxxxxxxxxxxxxxxxxxxxxxxxxxxxxxxxxxxx

How to Cook:

1. Add maple syrup and flour into a bowl. Mix well.

2. Add baking powder, salt, butter and milk. Blend until the texture is smooth.

3. Heat the oven to 300 F and prepare the baking dish.

4. Add the mixture in the baking dish and let it bake for 15 minutes.

5. When ready, serve and enjoy!

Recipe 21: Lemon Zest Muffins

Duration: 15 minutes

Serve: 2-3

Ingredient List:

- 2 tablespoons Butter
- ½ cup Sugar
- 2 cups Flour
- 2 tablespoons Lemon zest
- 1 Egg white
- 1 cup Milk
- 1 tablespoon Lemon juice
- Powdered sugar to garnish

xxxxxxxxxxxxxxxxxxxxxxxxxxxxxxxxxxxxxxxxxxxxxxxxxxxxxxxxx

How to Cook:

1. Heat the oven to 300 F and prepare the muffins oven proof bowls.

2. Add butter, sugar and flour into a bowl. Blend well.

3. Add lemon zest, egg white, and milk with lemon juice in it. Make sure the batter is without lumps.

4. Pour in the muffin bowls and let it bake for 15 minutes.

5. When done, garnish it with powdered sugar to serve!

Recipe 22: Almond Paste Puffs

Duration: 15 minutes

Serve: 2-3

Ingredient List:

- 2 cups Almond paste
- 1 cup Sugar
- ½ teaspoons Salt
- 4 tablespoons Amaretto liquor

How to Cook:

1. Add almond paste, sugar and salt with amaretto liquor into the bowl.

2. Blend well until the texture is smooth and without any lumps.

3. Heat the oven to 300 F and add a spoonful at equal distance on the baking tray.

4. Let it bake for 15 minutes.

5. When done, serve by sprinkling powdered sugar if desired.

Recipe 23: Melted Chocolate Bites

Duration: 15 minutes

Serve: 2-3

Ingredient List:

- 1 cup Butter
- 2 cups Flour
- ½ Vanilla bean
- 1 cup Almonds
- 2 cups Sugar
- ½ teaspoons Salt
- 4 Egg whites
- 2 tablespoons Orange zest
- 2 cups Chocolate (chopped)
- ½ cup Heavy cream

xxxxxxxxxxxxxxxxxxxxxxxxxxxxxxxxxxxxxxxxxxxxxxxxxxxxxxxxx

How to Cook:

1. Get a blender and crush the vanilla bean and almonds with flour.

2. Add to the bowl. Mix sugar, salt, egg whites and orange zest. Blend well.

3. Heat the oven to 300 F and prepare the baking tray.

4. Pour the mixture with equal distance and let it bake for 15 minutes.

5. On the other hand, melt chocolate on low heat and add heavy cream to it.

6. When the baking is done, take out the little bites and pour the melted chocolate on each bite.

7. Refrigerate for 20 minutes and serve when ready!

Recipe 24: Cupcakes with Nuts

Duration: 20 minutes

Serve: 2-3

Ingredient List:

- 2 cups Butter
- 2 cups Flour
- 2 tablespoons Sugar
- 1 tablespoon Brown sugar
- 3 Egg whites
- 1 tablespoon Baking powder
- 1 cup pistachios (chopped)
- 1 cup almonds (chopped)

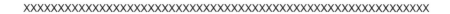

How to Cook:

1. Add butter, flour, sugar, brown sugar and baking powder into the bowl.

2. Whisk egg whites in a separate bowl and add to the mixture. Blend well.

3. Heat the oven to 400 F and pour the batter in the cupcakes tray.

4. Let it bake for 20 minutes.

5. When done, garnish it with chopped almonds and pistachios.

Recipe 25: Black Cherry Baked Dessert

Duration: 10 minutes

Serve: 2-3

Ingredient List:

- 2 tablespoons Butter
- 1 cup Milk
- 2 tablespoons Sugar
- 2 tablespoons Kirsch
- 2 tablespoons Vanilla extract
- 3 Eggs
- ¼ tablespoons Salt
- 2 cups Flour
- 2 cups Black cherries
- Powdered sugar for dusting

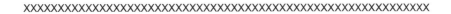

xxxxxxxxxxxxxxxxxxxxxxxxxxxxxxxxxxxxxxxxxxxxxxxxxxxxxxxxxxx

How to Cook:

1. Heat the oven to 300 F and prepare the baking tray.

2. Add butter, milk, sugar, kirsch, vanilla extract, eggs and salt in a bowl. Blend well.

3. Mix salt and flour. Make sure the batter is smooth.

4. Pour it into the baking tray and top the black cherries on it to bake for 10 minutes.

5. When ready, garnish with powdered sugar and serve!

Recipe 26: Crispy Creamy Pastries

Duration: 20 minutes

Serve: 2-3

Ingredient List:

- 2 cups Milk
- 1 tablespoon Vanilla bean extract
- 3 Egg yolks
- 2 tablespoons Sugar
- 2 tablespoons Cornstarch
- 3 tablespoons Butter
- 2 Puff pastry sheets
- ½ cup Confectioners' sugar

xxxxxxxxxxxxxxxxxxxxxxxxxxxxxxxxxxxxxxxxxxxxxxxxxxxxxxxxxxxx

How to Cook:

1. Mix milk, vanilla bean and egg yolks into a bowl.

2. Add sugar, cornstarch, butter and confectioners' sugar. Combine well.

3. Heat the oven to 300 F and bake the puff pastry sheets for 20 minutes.

4. When done, take out the sheets and cut them into squares.

5. Add the mixture to it and place the squares on top of each other.

6. When ready, serve and enjoy the crispy pastries.

Recipe 27: Simple Chocolate Puffs

Duration: 4 minutes

Serve: 2-3

Ingredient List:

- ½ cup Cold water
- ½ teaspoons Salt
- 2 cups Flour
- 2 cups Bread flour
- 2 cups Butter
- 3 tablespoons Cocoa powder

How to Cook:

1. Heat the oven to 300 F and prepare the baking tray.

2. Add flour, salt, water, bread flour and butter into a bowl.

3. Blend it with an electric blender for 3 minutes. Add cocoa powder.

4. Make sure there is no lump in the batter.

5. Pour the batter into the baking tray and let it bake for 20 minutes.

6. When done, enjoy the delicious chocolate patties.

Recipe 28: Lemon Zest Mousse

Duration: 20 minutes

Serve: 2-3

Ingredient List:

- 2 Eggs
- 2 teaspoons Sugar
- ¼ tablespoons Salt
- 2 tablespoons Lemon zest
- 2 cups Heavy cream
- 1 tablespoon Vanilla extract

xxxxxxxxxxxxxxxxxxxxxxxxxxxxxxxxxxxxxxxxxxxxxxxxxxxxxxxx

How to Cook:

1. Whisk eggs in a bowl.

2. Add sugar, salt, lemon zest, heavy cream and vanilla extract to the whisked eggs.

3. Place it in the fridge for 20 minutes.

4. When it settles, serve and enjoy the delicious mousse.

Recipe 29: Tasty Choco Mousse

Duration: 20 minutes

Serve: 2-3

Ingredient List:

- 1 cup Heavy cream
- 2 tablespoons Vanilla extract
- ½ tablespoons Salt
- 3 Egg whites
- 1 cup Sugar
- 2 cups Chocolate (chopped)
- Chocolate shavings to garnish

xxxxxxxxxxxxxxxxxxxxxxxxxxxxxxxxxxxxxxxxxxxxxxxxxxxxxxxxx

How to Cook:

1. Add heavy cream, vanilla extract, salt and sugar into a bowl.

2. Whisk egg whites in a separate bowl and add to the mixture.

3. Add the chopped chocolate and mix well.

4. Refrigerate for 20 minutes.

5. When ready, garnish with chocolate shavings to serve!

Recipe 30: Creamy Raspberry Dessert

Duration: 15 minutes

Serve: 2-3

Ingredient List:

- 1 cup Heavy cream
- 1 cup Sugar
- 3 cups Raspberries
- ½ cup Demerara sugar

xxxxxxxxxxxxxxxxxxxxxxxxxxxxxxxxxxxxxxxxxxxxxxxxxxxxxxx

How to Cook:

1. Get a large flat bowl and add heavy cream with sugar. Mix well.

2. Now, place the raspberries and blend gently.

3. Sprinkle the demerara sugar and refrigerate it for 15 minutes.

4. When ready, serve and enjoy!

Author's Afterthoughts

I can't appreciate you enough for spending your precious time reading my book. If there is anything that gladdens an author's heart, it is that his or her work be read. And I am extremely joyous that my labor and the hours put into making this publication a reality didn't go to waste.

Another thing that gladdens an author's heart is feedback because every comment from the good people who read one's book matters a great deal in helping you become better at what you do.

This is why I wouldn't shy away from reading your thoughts and comments about what you have read in this publication.

Do you think it is good enough? Do you think it could be better?

Please keep the feedback coming in, I won't hesitate to read any of them!!!

Thanks!

Layla Tacy

Biography

Climbing up the ladder from a young girl who loved to experiment with food items in her mother's cottage kitchen at the tender age of 7, to changing cooking from what it was to what it should be; Layla has more than made a name for herself, but she has created a dynasty for herself in the cooking world.

With more than twenty-five years in the culinary world, Layla has grown to be an authority with her influence spreading all over different high-class hotels and restaurants in and around Kansas City, such as Hilton President Kansas City, The Fountaine hotel, and Embassy Suites.

After working as a chef in different establishments, Layla moved on to become a chef-trainer to several up-and-coming chefs. Currently, she has graduated more than 200 trainees at her Chef School and presently has about 150 graduates in her school.

Made in the USA
Monee, IL
14 December 2021

85252344R00044